Skating on the Sky

Selected Poems

Claudia Walters Reinhardt

INFUSIONMEDIA

Lincoln, NE

INFUSIONMEDIA
140 North 8th Street #214
Lincoln, NE 68508-1353
www.infusion.media

ISBN: 978-0-9964283-2-3
First Edition
10 9 8 7 6 5 4 3 2 1
LCCN: 2015956749

Cover photo of sandhill cranes by Mark Davis reprinted with permission from the Omaha *World-Herald*. All other photos by Claudia Reinhardt.

I am grateful to the editors of the print and online journals and anthologies for publishing my work, including earlier versions of some of the poems in this book: *The Avocet Journal of Nature Poetry, Boneshaker Almanac, Contemporary Haibun Online, Colorado Life, Fox Cry Review, Illuminations, Nebraska Life, Owen Wister Review, Plains Song Review, The 2River View, The Wisconsin Review, Writing in Community* (Writelife); *The Untidy Season: Anthology of Nebraska Women Poets* (Backwaters Press), *Mother Nature's Trail, Celebrate XIX: A Collection of Writings by and about Women.*

For JR

CONTENTS

Everything is blooming most recklessly; if it were voices instead of colors, there would be an unbelievable shrieking into the heart of the night.

—**RAINER MARIA RILKE**

Spring

THE FIRST PEONY

Each year around Mom's birthday
as spring melted into summer,
Dad would come in from the garden
reverently bearing the season's first peony—
a bloom as brief as their love was long.
Mom would turn from the sink, dry her hands, and act surprised
as he presented the pink and white gift.
No words of endearment to make her blush.
No waltz around the kitchen to make us kids laugh.
Simply a single flower, shyly opening its heart—
the blossom's fragrance floating between them
as it passed from his farmer's hands to her accepting fingers.

COWBOY TAN

A battered hat brim shades faded, sky-blue eyes;
his moon-pale forehead and saddle-leather cheeks are separated by
a hedge of grizzled brows,
tangled as a pile of brush
marking the high water line
of the Eagle River's spring rise.

CARDINAL IN APRIL

Caught in the clutches of a flowering crab tree,
a cardinal flutters like a wild bandana torn from
the throat of a farmer climbing into the soundproof
cell of his tractor. The green machine rumbles
over ridges of moist soil, dripping chemicals
between earth's parted lips. Along the fence row,
the redbird sings as if just this morning
he remembered the tune
to the color of spring.

BURIED DEEP (HAIBUN)

The solitary oak guards a corner of prairie pasture: an aged warrior
rooted in deep prairie soil—survivor of blizzards, lightning, and hail.
I stand in the shade of its sheltering limbs and touch the shadow of
a hidden battle—twisted wire jutting from massive trunk. Generations
ago a farmer stretched new fence around a sapling. The tree grew;
strands tightened, cutting deeper and deeper. As barbs pressed into
its wrinkled breast, the oak embraced the invader, encircling pain
with layers of time, daring to grow taller, stronger, straighter.
A similar scar marks my breast—covered but not forgotten.
As another year circles by each spring,
it oozes the sap of incurable fear.

> *a wounded, wild heart*
> *buries, conceals, resists, and*
> *reaches for the sky*

SKATING ON THE SKY

Like a skater's flashing blade, a silver jet slashes across
a pool of endless blue, trailing a stream of vapor
above the Platte River—that ever-shrinking ribbon,
winding through the memory of an ancient valley.
Spring thermals bubble up from warming farm fields
ruffling the wings of ten thousand migrating cranes.
Their kettling vortex spirals higher and higher
until the swirling power of their collective joy
bends into a single, soaring plume—
an icy feather dancing on the surface of space

*Green was the silence, wet was the light, the month of June
trembled like a butterfly....*

—PABLO NERUDA

SUMMER

ASPEN ESCAPE (HAIBUN)

Along a mountain trail, two hikers step from searing sun into an aspen oasis.
Leaves, green as katydids, flutter past sunburned cheeks and sweaty shoulders
to alight on bulging backpacks: camouflage flirting with camouflage. Furry mosses
nap in the laps of trees. Slippery roots intertwine across the path: a cat's cradle
connecting ancestor to offspring: tree to tree to tree. A single, spreading being,
whose breath twirls leaves into tiny echoes of the circling eagle overhead.
The path twists and turns, rising sharply. Pale aspen faces bend closer;
knot-hole eyes follow the hikers.

> *escape through clinging*
> *veil of dappled shade into*
> *the afternoon sun*

ABANDONED BLOSSOMS

The gravel road dead-ends at a yard—
empty, except for cement steps leading nowhere,
like a tombstone marking the plot where a farmhouse
stood for generations, until last June when clouds swirled
green across the pasture; a tornado clawed open the roof
and ripped up the house by its roots. Weeks later,
a bulldozer buried the remains—
shredded curtains, shattered china, a twisted trophy—
the debris of dreams, abandoned by a family
that couldn't weather the sadness. Left behind,
the bulbs slept underground in their shelters
where the farm wife had gently laid them. Deep down,
she knew the flowers were extravagant, existing only
to be briefly beautiful; but she planted them anyway
to brighten the path from back porch to barn door.
The house now gone; people moved on,
but the forgotten flowers survived. And this spring,
the daffodils pushed through dark soil near the stairs.
Their ruffled trumpets, yellow as a lark's breast,
exploded into the chill air.

CROSSED FLIGHT PATHS

Brief as a blink, a flame with wings flashed across the gravel trail;
its shadow, a dark afterthought, skimmed the ground.
My bike skidded to a stop; I squinted in the morning sun
wondering ... where did it go? In answer, a chuckling call
tumbled through tangled branches, like the sound of water
trickling over stones. Two creatures—one grounded one free—
crossed paths: me, spinning over the earth, scattering
feathers of dust; the oriole, soaring through pools of light,
trailing a ribbon of song. Quick as a gasp, it was gone:
like the glimpse of a long-ago love,
disappearing into a thicket of people,
leaving only the memory of his smile.
No backward glance. No answering cry.
Cradling questions in a nest of empty hands,
I searched the sky for another chance
and yearned to someday fly.

BROWN THRESHER DOWNLOAD

Hidden in a thicket at the edge of a soybean field,
a brown thresher shuffles its playlist—
an avian collection, musical mash-up at thresher speed,
a thousand borrowed riffs from a rainbow repertoire:
goldfinch, indigo bunting, purple martin, cardinal.
Some melodies name the composer:
killdeer, catbird, bobwhite, chickadee.
Imitation, a sincere form of flattery, mockery, or larceny:
Snatch and sing
snatch and sing
and sing and sing and sing.

PRAYING PREYING MANTIS

I am surrounded by seen and unseen creatures
that creep, crawl, and slither
as I weed, pick, and prune plants
rooted in rich soil, home to sacred spirits
eons before I claimed this space as garden.
Kneeling beneath a canopied clematis,
I feel a sneaking fear and turn to peer
into the alien eyes of a praying mantis:
dragon of the insect world, phylum arthropoda.
Suspended from a star-white blossom,
body like a pea pod, jaws still chewing,
perhaps the head of her mate—
consumed while consummating.
People call it savage; she would say survival.
Her folded front legs suddenly raise in penitence,
or praise. Her monstrous head twists to gaze past
my human intrusion, into a higher kingdom
where she is seen as beautiful,
and the season is always spring.

FAMILY

FISHING LESSON (HAIBUN)

"You're not up North 'til you hear the loon call," Dad said, as he grasped a squirming worm. "If you're going to fish, you've got to bait your own hook." Three pairs of blue eyes stared. In a boat loaded with anticipation, we clutched bamboo fishing poles that quivered like compass needles, pointing us to the Flambeau Flowage each summer. Three giggling girls in puffy life vests, learning to be patient predators and cast without snagging a sister. No splashing. No dragging fingers in the water. Watch the bobber. Watch and wait. Watch and wait. We wished for fish as the rocking boat lulled us into silence. Time floated on waves. We drifted. I dreamed of a birch-bark canoe gliding along the shoreline.

Loon's yodeling call
echoes northern summertime
feathered water spirit

GRANDMA'S HANDS

I remember her summer-light touch on my head
as we walked from the house to the barn.
She wore a thin, gold wedding band;
no bracelet-encircled wrists;
no polish on her fingertips.
Her hands were scarred from a life of labor
as farm wife, midwife, neighbor, and mother;
she could crimp the edge of a cherry pie
or snap the neck of a Rhode Island Red
—mud, blood, feathers, bone—
then pluck it and fry it for dinner.
Her fingers flew at quilting bees,
picked and shelled spring green peas,
dug potatoes
canned tomatoes
put up peaches and beets,
slopped the hogs
stacked up logs
and made a harmonica sing.
I never saw her hands at rest,
even at last in a nursing home:
eyes closed and alone, her curled fingers
stroking the blanket's furrowed field.

GRANDPA'S TWO-FINGERED WAVE

The clover-colored Chevy tugged a parachute of dust along
a gravel road lined by telephone wires, fragile as veins
connecting neighbors across cornfields and pastures.
Riding to town with Grandpa, I was barely tall enough
to stretch a brown arm out the window, fingers fanned
to comb the scent of summer from the passing breeze.
I clenched a toothpick in my teeth—like Grandpa;
except not all of his teeth were real. I'd wondered—
but never asked—about the pink and white crescent
smiling in a glass of water by his bed at night.
Grandpa gripped the wheel with fingers thick from
too many mornings milking cows and birthing lambs;
his speckled hands more accustomed to driving a team
of horses in a bean field than a cranky car on a gravel road.
At the one-lane bridge over Hurricane Creek,
we pulled over to let a neighbor cross; and as his truck
rattled by, the driver lifted two fingers off the wheel.
Grandpa returned the greeting—a slow motion
that spoke of shared fence lines, common hardships,
and knowledge that their time was passing.

RIVER SISTERS

Riding the Wisconsin River in her blue kayak,
my silver-haired sister leans back to coast on
the breath between strokes. As the eldest, she
was always the one who led, scouting a path in
the world ahead, following an inner compass,
sending back lessons the rest of us were too young
to understand. On this winding waterway, we drift in
her silent wake, baptized by a sprinkle of maple seeds.
Our paddles dip and swirl tiny tempests that recede
into the deep current of memory. Three lives entwined
like the roots of trees, bending low in the summer breeze
to ripple the river with their fingertips.

SOWING ADVICE

"Sow above-ground crops in a waxing moon and
below-ground crops in a waning moon,"
Grandma said, brushing back strands of silver hair
and fanning the humid, buzzing air. Leaning on the
weathered hoe, its handle as sturdy as her spirit,
she tried to advise me—girl who lived at city pace
in too big a hurry to understand the world
could wear down even the strongest sower.
She shared sayings and stories; but I thought
I knew about living and dying and growing.
Now I'd give the moon to be in her garden again;
I would listen closely as Grandma reminisced
about how she had sown in hardship
and still reaped happiness.

FALL

MILKWEED POD

Between dusty road and sagging fence
rustling prairie grasses surround
a solitary milkweed plant. Its silver-brown pods
curve like horse nostrils, flaring to catch
the scent of fall, then exhaling a
silken cloud that drifts over rippling pastures,
whispering of butterflies and passing seasons.

ALL GONE SOUTH

Dawn breaks later and later, until one September morning
I wake to an alarming silence. No buntings, kingbirds, or swallows,
no martins, warblers, or wrens sing. When the sun shrugs off
her shroud of fog, only dry leaves flutter in the north wind.
If I had known their departure date, I'd have saved
their summer songs, hidden them under my pillow.
But, like you, they slipped away,
leaving while I dreamed.
No warning note, no final call.
Now I face the chill of fall
without the thrill of wings.

HAWK AND SNAKE (HAIBUN)

Coast through clouds, hover over sagebrush, focus on movement, float lower.
Black and brown diamonds slide over rocks. Snake weaves between
stealth and silence, wedged head lifting, eyes fixed. I dive, beating the air:
my element. Swooping low, shadow racing ahead as if to warn. Too late.
Claws clench. Snake coils, recoils, belly exposed. I flap and hop, flap and hop,
pinning spine to ground. Snake thrashes, lashing my body. Beak rips flesh,
talons tighten, wings extend, lift into the sky. Snake twists and twirls,
reaching for one last touch of earth. Soar higher, waiting for death—
circling until the limp body signals it's safe to land and feed.

touching only earth
element of air unknown
dying while flying

Sun on my back, belly on soil. Movement ahead. Tongue flutters, seeking scent:
in and out; in and out. Raising my head, crawling toward the body heat of prey.
I feel a chill of shadow, then stabbing, grabbing fangs, my armor punctured
by pain. Open mouth strikes only air. Coil and recoil. My full length, full strength,
beating the body above me. Dragged from the earth: my element. I twist and
stretch, touching nothing but nothingness, feeling only the wind of wing beats.
Smell of ground—gone. Limp spine lengthens. Hawk circles a pile of sticks,
drifting down to tiny clumps of feathers—beaks agape, red throats waiting.

CICADA CHILDREN

Along a gravel road, the cottonwoods
lift their long limbs and sway in dusty rhythm,
cheering the rock concert of cicadas
whose cyclic song starts slowly,
a solo buzz of grating tymbals,
then crescendos to a pulsating thrum—
like a thousand bug-eyed children,
circling a playground
gyrating with joy
vibrating their tiny wings
shrieking, "Look at me!" "Look at me!"

FALL EQUINOX

The seasons pause in perfect symmetry:
daylight and dark, sunset and moonrise
connected across horizon's arc.
For months, tall grasses have leaned away
from summer's steamy breath; now they stretch
and straighten in cool air and unfurl plumes that
float like hair on water. Waves of swallows swirl
the space between dawn and dusk.
As the wind shifts its weight to the north,
a necklace of geese spills from the clouds,
softly tugging the blue cloak of night across
the prairie's sloping shoulders.
Seasons balance:
daylight recedes, darkness advances,
and fall creeps into the nest where summer slept.

One kind word can warm three months of winter.

—JAPANESE PROVERB

WINTER

SUNDOG DECEPTION

The winter sun radiated deception—all light, no heat—
through a farmhouse window, enticing the little girl
to sneak behind her mother's back and
venture out in brittle air to stare at
shimmering wisps of rainbow:
a sundog—fusion of fire, ice and fog,
like a cosmic secret floating near the sun.
Then the solar colors shifted,
showering confetti crystals that sifted
through the vapor of her breath and
lit an icy halo in her flaming hair,
as she ran inside to breakfast
before her mother knew she wasn't there.

FIRST NIGHT OF SKATING SEASON (HAIBUN)

Funnels of light dangle over our backyard ice rink, luring the neighborhood tribe.
Children rummage through the box of last year's leftovers, digging like badgers
to find skates that fit. Tattered hats and mismatched mittens can't muffle
the excitement as we stumble along the path to the pond—a glowing opal,
draped in drifts of glittering scarves. We fly and slip from crack-the-whip,
novices held up or pushed down. Smiles bright as blades. Cries of laughter
circle the moon while December's dark breath numbs noses and toes.
Waltzing through a blizzard of children, my ballerina mother spins a perfect
figure eight. A cloud of music floats up to our bedroom window where my
pretty preteen sister, torso bound in snow-white plaster, watches and waits
for the dance of her loving life to begin.

radiating cold
melted by children's laughter
community warms

APPROACHING DENVER ON A WINTER AFTERNOON

The jet soars over mounds of churning clouds
lower and lower
until it skims the rumpled blanket of plains,
as if the earth—restless with snow dreams—
had tossed and turned all night, only to wake
to an achingly cold dawn. Across the aisle,
a petite woman with possum-gray hair and
her arm in a sling struggles to raise the shade.
The plane noses into the stiff wind, racing for the runway.
I peer out through a skiff of snow and see below,
a coyote trotting along a creek bed, nose sifting
icy scents, intent—like me—on reaching home
before the storm begins to howl.

EMBARRASSED BY MY CAT

Clouds huddled on the horizon, hiding from the clawing wind
as I came home to find a slumbering lump in the bed.
My blue-eyed cat had taken refuge from the cold floor
and crawled beneath a quilt made by my grandmother,
a strong-willed farm woman who believed
"animals should earn their keep" and "cats belong outside."
Years ago, she'd pieced torn shirts and worn dresses
into the patchwork now covering my pampered pet.
With a rush of shame, I scolded the cat,
who slunk from under the coverlet and sat
yawning and blinking, then stretched and gazed at me
as if to say he had just-this-moment come inside
after catching mice in the barn all day.

GEESE IN WINTER

I hear them before I see them;
their ancient calls resonate in icy air.
Pushed by a west wind, the birds
flee the sunset's red explosion.
The shifting wedge banks overhead
so close I hear their soft sighs and see their bellies,
the same shades as snow and grass and cornhusks.
Their slender necks reach to the darkening east—
tracing ancient sky paths, searching for nighttime shelter,
guided by a memory of places long ago safe.
For a moment, I hear single calls, see separate wings;
they merge into a wavering thread,
tethering sunset to nightfall
and winter to spring.

Mitakuye Oyasin (Lakota)
"We are all related."

PEOPLE, COMMUNITY, WORLD

CROW FEATHER WOMAN

Torn from a wing that stroked the wind's back,
a feather so black it sheds light like water—
fragment of a bold scolding bird,
once member of a dancing flock:
a murder of crows, murmuring to each other.
Torn from a soaring body, a single pinion
caught in the claws of a prairie rose bush,
fluttering
but not flying.

Hair once black as raven's wing, Crow woman
of the Whistling Waters clan, Absaroka tribe,
called "children of the large-beaked bird."
In the shawl dance, her braided ropes of night
flew free: now feathered with gray, resting on
shoulders, bent but not beaten by years
of injustice, caught between cultures:
drifting
between earth and sky.

SOUND OFF

On the silent screen
I see a silver casket;
people huddle near an open wound in the grass.
Like flowers seeking sun, their faces turn
toward a tall man with eyes dark as his beard.
He lifts a hand to calm the air;
but I hear no sound, only the emptiness
between words as he pauses to breathe.
Maybe he speaks of life and love lost,
a heart's cadence stilled.
No sound. No answer.
Bodies recoil at the gunshots;
the honor guard reloads.
Smoke unfurls a flag across the sky,
saluting the space between words
and breaths
and thoughts.
In the silence, only the echo of loss remains.

ECHO OF SHAKING HANDS

In the spotlight,
the violinist bent and swayed,
a fragile puppet straining against strings.
Her cheek nestled on a shoulder of amber wood;
her hand curled around the slender throat,
fingers shaking and aching with passion for
music that poured forth like light into air.

In the shadowy balcony, a man rested,
eyes closed, white head swaying,
fingers playing along the curve of a cane.
His knotted hands ached from the illness
that stole his touch but not his feeling
for the music that resonated within.

In the final movement,
their fingers played a duet,
each reaching for the last note—
hers a soaring vibrato,
his a silent echo.
For a moment, their unacquainted souls
folded together in harmony,
then opened to the thunder
from thousands of clapping hands.

EVENING IN SHANGHAI

From the hotel window, I peer across an urban canyon to a gray building:
balconies festooned with trousers and blouses—flapping in the dank breeze.
A pigeon coop perches on one balcony, a cage filled with murmuring birds.
As neon lights blossom along the street, cars, trucks, and motorcycles flow
like fish sauce through tangled noodles—slow progress punctuated by
sputtering engines, jangling horns, whistles of white-gloved police. In the alley,
an old man squats near a small fire. Smells mingle: oil from his cook pot,
cigarettes, exhaust, garbage. The odors waft up, floating past the balcony
where a thin woman reaches into the cage and grabs a plump pigeon.
A casual snap of her wrist; the bird goes limp. Clutching its pink feet,
she carries the body inside.

silent pigeons wait
far below growling traffic
pushes back the night

OVERHEARD IN THE DOCTOR'S OFFICE

In the corner by the window, two women lean in like willows,
white curls nearly entwined, pastel sweaters draped over shoulders
to ward off the swirling chill of anxiety. One grips the handles of a walker,
the other fans her face with a worn magazine.
Their soft words drift back and forth like a porch swing.

> *Look—a recipe for cherry walnut cake.*
>
> *My, that sounds good right now.*
>
> *Grace used to make the best cherry walnut cake,*

but she's crippled up now; can't get out much.

> *I heard her son's in trouble again.*
>
> *Again? My son knew him in high school—handsome kid,*

had a wild streak: women, rodeo, job in the oil fields.

> *Gracie did the best she could, raising those kids alone.*

And I know what being alone's like.

> *Her daughter moved to Omaha; doesn't want Gracie driving anymore.*
>
> *But she only goes to the doctor's and Walmart. I get my jam and jelly at Walmart.*
>
> *Do they have apple butter there? My Jim loved apple butter;*

haven't had apple butter since he passed on.

> *Funny, you don't think about things like that—'til they're gone.*

NATURE

BE TURQUOISE (HAIBUN)

I want to be turquoise: hydrous phosphate of copper and aluminum—
artisans' medium for mosaic domes and talismans. Turquoise—
from deep teal to pale mint—coveted on every continent; birthed in earth's
most arid regions, each fragment a fingerprint of geologic memory.

> *desert oasis*
> *color of ancient dreams*

I want to spin the global color wheel, creating all shades of sea—
marine, cerulean, azure, aqua—reflecting the flash of hummingbird throat
and dragonfly wing; submerged in senses—whisper of wind, scent of water,
taste of tears, touch of mystery.

> *rain dancing legends*
> *color of ceremony*

I want to be robin's egg blue for millennia—hue of heaven and earth:
not blue, not green, yet both. Turquoise: a chromatic chameleon and
kaleidoscopic story told in sky-stone, precious celestial gem—
elemental source of clarity, acuity, and perception.

> *timeless patina*
> *color of tranquility*

SCOLDING A GOLDFINCH

Where were you going, dandelion with wings,
when you tried to pierce the window that
divides earthbound and airborne?
Bravado brought you here—
imprisoned in my nested hands—
your golden body light as milkweed,
wings shuttered like fans,
claws tight as a baby's fist,
heart fluttering against my palm.
Inside, my cat watches, tail twitching.
Outside, I watch, dead-still with awe
until your black eyes snap open with a focus so fierce
they force my fingers to open like petals,
releasing an explosion of sunshine,
leaving behind the cat and me to wonder:
who is captive and who is free?

EGRET IN THE SHALLOW END (HAIBUN)

Florida dawn, air thick as mud. I step outside, peer down at the egg-shaped
swimming pool. An egret—the color of snow it's never seen—stands motionless.
One leg punctures the ripples; the other dangles scaly toes. Yellow dagger beak
poised to stab; snaking neck ready to swallow. Predator on a futile mission.
Old lessons—find water, find food—no longer true. Egrets came within a feather
of extinction: sacrificing breeding plumage for ladies hats, a dangerous coupling
of sex and style. Lawn sprinklers sprout like mushrooms. Water clarified with
chemicals. Salinity rises; fresh water sinks. No frog-filled, stinky swamp;
no bottom-creeping crawfish; no silver finny minnows—only dizzy water bugs.
This wading warrior adapted to the artificial;
like us, blind to the truth flowing around him.

seeping salt water
oozing and undrinkable
no nest is safe

RIFFING ON GREEN

With apologies to Wallace Stegner

Between blue and yellow on the spectral rainbow,
is a secondary color, both mellow and sensational.
We sing about trees of green and places where the
grass grows all around, all around. The world seems
filled with chlorophyll; still it's not easy being green.

Green is contradictory, yin and yang, a two-sided story.
Is it old as Eden or young as spring? Healthy and growing
or ill around the gills? Eco-friendly or rotting and moldy?
Greenhouse gases or green-thumbed people growing
food for the masses? Does it mean jealousy and envy
or verdant pasture of opportunity?

All our senses perceive a greenly tinge in the
smell of fresh-cut clover, burning cedar, forest glen;
sound of pond-dwelling bullfrog or stalking night heron;
feel of slimy okra, prickly pear, tickly fern;
taste of pickled peppers, hot chilies, cold watermelon.

Green grows in every season:
spring asparagus, spinach, and peas
summer basil, zucchini, and beans
fall collards, kale, and broccoli

winter's thorny mistletoe, holly, and ivy.
The word means unripe or unseasoned; but we
savor green seasonings: parsley, sage, rosemary, thyme.

A dozen green pigments on my mother's painter's palette;
some hues melt to yellow, others fade to blue:
citron, celadon, jade and malachite. Tubes ooze their
color-essence until each name becomes the tint:
avocado, olive, emerald, pine, and mint.

Green beings thrive on land, in air and sea:
neon gecko, moray eel, and floating clumps of algae,
iridescent damselfly, luminescent lightning bug,
midnight sheen of loon head, moonlight luna moth.

I could hike meadow and forest each day
and still not get over the color green.
I cannot live without wild green spaces
or even those briefly greenish places;
green is the spirit of earthly grace,
and green restores my soul.

ANGLE OF LIGHT

Earth serenely spins in bright infinity,
axis tipping imperceptibly—
altering the angle of light,
shifting day and night,
changing everything.

In Appreciation to

My mother, Adrienne Jean Roscoe Walters, born in 1920: She celebrated creativity, shared her artistic talent, and passed on her love of reading and education. She was a teacher who enjoyed children, embraced a global perspective, and encouraged respect for others.

My father: Jake Alexander Walters, born in 1918: He grew up on a small farm and became a World War II pilot. He loved his family and enjoyed nature, sports, and music—especially singing in the church choir. He could recite poems he had memorized as a child in a one-room school.

My sisters: Cynthia Diane Walters Owen and Linda Elaine Walters Young, whose enduring love and laughter have inspired and supported me in many ways.

Many extended family members, friends, teachers, and colleagues.

In her dreams, she rides wild horses
And they carry her away on the wind
And they never make a sound
As they fly above the ground.
Tonight, she rides wild horses, again.

"She Rides Wild Horses"
Lyrics by Bob Corbin and Ted Hewitt

CPSIA information can be obtained at www.ICGtesting.com
Printed in the USA
LVIW01n2345070116
469711LV00003B/4